The 'ten rules' concept sets out to be gently provocative. Sadly, the 'rules' in this booklet are reflective of many of the practices we have come across that cause so many problems for people with learning disabilities who are on the autism spectrum, and those who care for and support them, often leading to miscommunication on both sides of conversation.

We hope it will be a useful starting point for discussion and a catalyst for action.

'Three things in human life are important. The first is to be kind. The second is to be kind. The third is to be kind.'

Henry James

A note on terminology

In this booklet, the term autistic people has been used rather than person with autism, in recognition of the term preferred by autistic people.

Introduction

This publication (like those in the same series) is based on the premise that autism is diverse. It is therefore helpful to try and understand a person's communication and interaction by thinking about how each person is likely to see, experience and interpret the world. This will help those who care for or support autistic people who have learning disabilities to better understand how to communicate and enable staff and carers to offer help and support around communication, which is based on a deeper understanding of each person's strengths and needs.

Each 'rule' acts as a useful starting point for discussion and a catalyst for action. It is followed by suggestions for positive practices. The booklet also contains further background information on concepts and sources of information, together with references.

The booklet can be used for a wide range of purposes, including staff induction, autism awareness training, individual professional development and reflection, and team discussions regarding service development and design.

What are the communication experiences of autistic people who have learning disabilities?

Our research at the Tizard Centre (Bradshaw *et al*, 2016) has found that autistic people who have learning disabilities are:

- Less likely to be engaged in activities, with people engaged in activities for only just over one third of the time. This means that people had long periods of time with nothing to do.

- Less likely to be receiving skilled support.

- Less likely to have contact from staff with people spending, on average, nearly 80% of their time with no contact from staff.

We also looked at how the autistic people who had learning disabilities communicated. We found that:

- Half of the autistic people were described as being non-verbal.

- Most of the people described as being non-verbal did not have any formal means of non-verbal communication available to them (e.g. signed communication or symbols).

- Only a quarter of people were described as having communication that was effective all of the time.

- Nearly 15% of people were described by staff as not understanding verbal communication.

We also observed how staff communicated:

- Staff communication was most likely to be verbal, even with people who staff told us did not understand verbal communication.

- A small number of people did not have any communication directed to them at all during the time of our observation.

- Only a small number of communication exchanges were supported by visual communication such as signed communication, symbols, photographs or signs.

Though we saw some very good examples of communication, which had been adapted to take into account the needs and preferences of people being supported, many autistic people who had learning disabilities experienced poor communication. For a number of people, communication was infrequent and poorly adapted to individuals' needs.

Difficulties in social communication and interaction form a major part of the diagnostic criteria for autism, alongside 'repetitive behaviours and interests'. Often however, such problems are seen as purely the fault of the autistic person and their way of trying to interact and communicate, rather than a mutual interactive issue for both parties (Milton, 2017). In this booklet, we propose ten rules of how best to miscommunicate with autistic people and people with learning disabilities…and maybe what to do about it!

The 'Ten rules' series was conceived by **Richard Mills** (Research Director, Research Autism and Hon. Research Fellow, University of Bath, Visiting Professor, Taisho University, Tokyo; Bond University, Australia) and **Dr Damian Milton** (Lecturer in intellectual and developmental disabilities, Tizard Centre, University of Kent). Other titles in the series can be found at www.pavpub.com.

Assume you know best

After all, you have a lot of experience of communicating, you do it all the time. You are bound to know what is going to work best for me.

Make sure you don't talk to my family or other people who know me well. After all, what would we/they know!

Positive practices

☺ Try to put yourself in my shoes and don't rely on assumptions from your own experience, as this is likely to be very different to mine.

☺ Talk to family and other people who know me well.

☺ Find out *what* I like to communicate about.

☺ Find out *how* I like to communicate.

☺ Find out *who* I like to communicate with. What do successful communication partners seem to do well?

☺ Think about the environment. It might make a big difference if I find the lighting too bright or if it's noisy or crowded. I might not be able to focus on communication and interaction at all.

☺ Take time to notice when communication is really successful (who, what, where, when, how?).

☺ Be open and flexible, prepared to make mistakes and learn from them.

Rule 2

Just use verbal communication with me at all the times

☢️ After all, that's what most people use to communicate and it works just fine.

☢️ If verbal communication doesn't seem to work the first time, say it again, louder, use more words, move closer to me (and just keep going).

Positive practices

☺ Find out from me or from people who know me well what the best forms of communication are.

☺ Many autistic people who have learning disabilities find it hard to understand speech and using other forms of communication (e.g. signs, symbols or objects) can help people to understand.

☺ Additional visual forms of communication can be really helpful as I can take my time to understand what is being communicated.

☺ Using signed communication, symbols, photos and objects of reference can help to remind me what we are communicating about.

☺ Be aware that hearing loss might be an issue for some people (and might not be recognised).

☺ Verbal communication on its own might be ok for me for some of the time but will be harder when I am feeling stressed or upset or cross.

☺ Using signed communication, symbols, photos and objects of reference can help to show me that you value different ways of communicating.

☺ If verbal communication does not seem to be helping, try other ways.

Rule 3

Use as many words as you can when you communicate with me

☢ It is always better to provide lots of details all the time and just keep speaking.

☢ If I look confused, then just keep going using more words as your message will get through to me in the end.

☢ Keep speaking and keep rephrasing things in as many different ways as possible.

Positive practices

- ☺ Less is often more! It is good idea to think about the key idea/s that you want to express and think about how to do that clearly.

- ☺ Start with the key idea and use simple language.

- ☺ You might want to start by communicating about what I am doing now rather than something I am going to be doing later.

- ☺ Give me time to process each piece of information before you give me more information to deal with.

- ☺ Silences are good. Too much verbal communication can just become 'noise' and instead of giving information, makes it even harder for me to process and understand.

- ☺ Give me time to ask questions.

- ☺ Provide structure to the interaction so that I know what to expect. Start by saying my name so that I know that you are taking to me. Make sure I know what the topic is. Make sure I know that I will be able to ask questions.

- ☺ If it is something very important, make sure I have all the information I need in another form too (written or symbols for example).

Rule 4
Always insist on eye contact

☢ After all if I am not looking at you, then I can't possibly be listening to you can I!

Positive practices

☺ Find other ways to work out whether or not I am ready to have a conversation with you.

☺ Make taking part in communication as easy as possible. Ask me (or other people who know me well) about what you can do to help me feel comfortable.

☺ Don't impose your views about what good eye contact might be and think about my individual preferences.

☺ Did you know that I sometimes find it easier to listen when I am not looking at you?

☺ Eye contact is sometimes uncomfortable or painful and stops me from listening to what is being said.

☺ Think about where you position yourself in relation to me. Can I easily make and break eye contact when I need to? Is it easier if we are side-by-side or diagonal rather than directly opposite one another?

☺ Perhaps provide something visual too so that we both have something to focus on. For example, if we are talking about planning the day, a diary or visual timetable might help. If we are working out what to cook, a cookery book or recipe cards might help.

Rule 5

Try to get a mismatch between your verbal and non-verbal communication

Make sure I can't decide whether I need to pay attention to what you say or what you are communicating with your non-verbal communication.

Positive practice

☺ Think about things from my perspective. I might have as much difficulty in reading your communication as you do reading mine!

☺ Other non-verbal communication (facial expression, tone of voice, body posture etc.) might be something I find hard to read. The more obvious you can make your communication, the easier I will find it.

☺ Ask me (or other people who know me well) what helps. I might need you to tell me how you are feeling rather than you relying on me reading your facial expression or tone of voice.

☺ Gestures are vague and difficult to understand. I might need more formal visual communication systems such as photos, signed communication and objects of reference.

☺ Don't make assumptions about my non-verbal communication. I might not look to you like I am upset or angry or happy or cross. You might find it hard to read my expressions.

Rule 6

Always be vague and obscure

☢ Never mean what you say or do as you say – be as confusing as possible.

☢ Even better, do this at the same time as rules 3, 4, 5 and 7.

Positive practice

☺ Avoid using sarcasm and irony unless we
  have built up a good rapport. Even then
  I might not like it. I might interpret what you
  say quite literally.

☺ Say what you mean and mean what you say.
  You might need to check with other people
  how best to present information clearly.

☺ Acknowledge a miscommunication when
  it happens.

☺ Be as predictable as you can. I will find it easier
  to take part if you provide clear information.

☺ Find a way to tell me how much information
  you need from me. Do you want a yes/no
  answer or more than that?

Insist on interacting with me whenever you want to and pay no attention to my actions or wishes

We all like to chat don't we and it is 'good for me' to socialise.

Positive practice

☺ Ask me (or other people who know me well) when communication is likely to be easier or more difficult.

☺ Do you like to be around noisy, bouncy, bubbly people? Perhaps I do too or maybe I find that quite difficult. Ask me (or other people who know me well) what my preferred interaction style is.

☺ There might be topics I really enjoy talking about. Perhaps you could find people who share my interests?

☺ I probably find it easier to interact when I feel more in control. Find ways that control can be shared by both of us.

☺ If I look like I am not interested in talking to you at the moment, see if you can find a better time.

☺ You might need to give me time to finish what I am doing before I am ready to talk to you. You could try asking me if you can come back in five minutes.

Rule 8

Ignore me

If you find me hard to interact with me, you could try ignoring me, especially if you think the way I am communicating is 'inappropriate'.

After all, autistic people don't like to chat do they, so best to leave me on my own.

Positive practice

☺ I might be just as confused about your way of communicating as you are about mine.

☺ I can probably interact better with people who have taken the time to build a relationship with me.

☺ Be predictable in your interactions with me.

☺ Think about times when I seem to prefer interaction and use those times to build the relationship.

☺ Think about what I might want and need. There might be times when I really do want to be on my own. This doesn't mean that I never want to interact with anyone.

☺ It is probably easier for you to change your behaviour than it is for me to change mine.

Rule 9

Demean me

Be derogatory to me, especially in your ways of communicating/acting socially. Make fun of the things that are important to me and laugh at any errors I make.

Positive practice

☺ Think about it from my point of view. I might have had many experiences of trying and getting things 'wrong'.

☺ Accept that I might have ways of interacting or behaving that are really important to me but that make no sense to you. (Guess what? Some of the ways you interact and behave make no sense to me either!)

☺ Find out what my strengths are and help me to use those.

☺ Don't make judgements about what I can and can't do. I might be really skilled at some aspects of communication even though I find other parts much more difficult.

☺ Be careful about the language you use to talk about the things I find difficult.

☺ Recognise that communication and interaction always involve more than one person and we share responsibility for successful communication.

Don't make any adaptations – just treat me the same as you treat everyone else

After all, I need to learn to fit in and be just the same as everyone else.

Positive practices

☺ Use communication strategies that work best with me. If you don't know what those strategies are, ask me or other people who know me well.

☺ If in doubt, follow these rules:

- Keep it clear and simple.

- Back up verbal communication with something visual (written words or symbols for example).

- Give me time.

- Make communication predictable.

- Learn from your mistakes.

- Share responsibility for communication.

- Say what you mean and mean what you say.

Further explanations

Rule 1: Assume you know best

Ever heard this phrase: 'If you have met one autistic person … you have met one autistic person'?

Some autistic people who have learning disabilities will communicate verbally. Other people may have a few words or phrases. Some people might use signs or symbols. Some people might use high tech communication aids (such as voice output communication aids) or an iPad with apps. Some autistic people who have learning disabilities might find it very difficult to communicate and might be very reliant on other people to interpret their needs and wishes.

Some autistic people might understand complex verbal communication. Other people might understand simple phrases. Some people might understand some very familiar key words. Other autistic people with learning disabilities might be very reliant on the context and situation to make sense of communication and what is being talked about.

It is a good idea to think about who communicates most successfully with the autistic person you are working with. Of course, some of that success in communication is likely to be built on good relationships but it is also likely to be because communication partners have worked out how to best communicate with that person.

When trying to empathise with autistic people, non-autistic people will draw upon their own experience to do so, and yet this may lead them astray, as their experience may well be very different to that of the person they are attempting to communicate with. As argued by Milton (2017) there can be a 'double empathy problem' in that both communication partners may have difficulty in understanding the other, their frame of reference, and predicting what they might do next. In order to not make false assumptions, it means being humble in one's interpretations and not quick to judge, and to build trust and rapport over time.

The positive strategies that are described in this book are likely to be good practice and generally helpful, and are often a good starting point.

It is really important to acknowledge expertise by experience, whether this is by getting information directly from the autistic person themselves or from family, or friends and people who know the autistic person well.

Rule 2: Just use verbal communication with me at all the times

Many autistic people who have learning disabilities find it harder to process and understand spoken words. If you think about it, once you have said the word, it is gone and there isn't a permanent reminder of the word that has been spoken. It is harder to process spoken communication when we are stressed. Have you ever been very worried? Ever been to see the doctor and come out and not been able to remember what he or she said? What about when you are feeling cross or upset? Does it help if people kept talking at you or did you find it hard to listen? Most people find it harder to process information during times of upset. Many autistic people will have difficulties processing spoken communication at least some of the time.

We all tend to rely on additional visual forms of communication at least some of the time. What do you do if you have lots to think about or a set of complex instructions to follow? You probably don't just try to remember everything. You probably write it down. However, not everybody can read.

Other more visual forms of communication e.g. photos, symbols, line drawings, objects of reference, signed communication (in addition to written words) can help. This is because you can keep looking at the image and take the time you need to process the information.

If you say something to an autistic person and the person doesn't seem to respond or understand, try a different way.

Remember that it is possible for someone to repeat the words that they hear without them necessarily understanding what has been said. Echoing (repeating) words and phrases might be a good strategy as it allows the person to 'join in' with the interaction. It might give the person the additional time they need to process what has been said. Don't assume understanding.

Talking Mats® (Murphy & Cameron, 2006) is a structured framework which uses visual symbols to support communication. Talking Mats might be used to explore a range of topics, such as things that people would like to do, places people would like to go, things that help good communication, sensory sensitivities etc. They can be a really good way of getting to know someone and their views (Murphy & Cameron, 2008). Talking Mats have also developed some guidelines on using this approach with autistic people: https://www.talkingmats.com/wp-content/uploads/2013/09/ASD-guidelines.pdf.

Rule 3: Use as many words as you can when you communicate with me

More words or different words or repeated words may not always help. You might just be creating more 'noise' and making it even more difficult for the person you are interacting with to understand you.

A common issue for autistic people is having difficulty processing lots of information at the same time from multiple sources. This can create sensory overload and fragmentation, leading to heightened stress and confusion.

It is a good idea to break up information so that you give the person time to process what you have said before you move on to say something else. Think about a time when you found something difficult. Did it help if people kept talking at you? Did that distract you from what you were trying to do? If people go too fast and keep adding more information, it is really easy to get lost (and sometimes to then give up!).

Less is often more, particularly if the individual is feeling stressed or upset. You might need to find alternative visual methods of communication (see Rule 2).

Some words are much more difficult to understand (e.g. time concepts, emotions, negatives or words such as 'not', 'don't' etc.). You might need to think about different ways of communicating these difficult concepts, for example:

- Saying what is happening rather than what isn't.

- Using symbols to help describe emotions.

- Using a visual timetable to help explain time concepts.

It is harder to understand when people talk about what has happened in the past or what is going to happen in the future. It is easier when people talk about what is actually happening now.

Some sentence structures are harder to process e.g. 'we are going swimming after we have been to the shops'. It would be simpler to rephrase this as 'we are shopping and then swimming'. People usually expect what they hear first to be the first thing that is happening.

It is important to remember that people might not have a way of telling you that they haven't understood what you said.

Rule 4: Always insist on eye contact

Do you always make good eye contact when you are interacting? Do you sometimes find it easier not to make eye contact, e.g. when you are having a difficult conversation? It is sometimes easier to have a difficult conversation when you are in a car and have to keep your eyes on the road rather than looking at the person you are talking to. Eye contact is **not** essential for effective communication and sometimes makes interaction and communication more difficult.

For some autistic people, it is always easier to listen if they are not making eye contact. Some autistic people find it uncomfortable or even painful to make eye contact. It is important to recognise individual preferences and not impose your views. The more comfortable the autistic person is, the more they are likely to be able to communicate.

Autistic people might be looking near your eyes (for example, at the bridge of your nose) or making brief glances. Autistic people might find it difficult to understand 'rules' around when to make eye contact and how long for. Autistic people might find it difficult to integrate eye contact with other elements of communication and interaction. (An alternative viewpoint is of course that autistic people just have different ways of interacting and communicating and we need to understand these different ways.)

If you are looking at someone when they are interacting with you, it might help you to notice some parts of communication and interaction that can help you to interpret messages. For example, facial expressions can change when people are using sarcasm and irony or saying something intended to be humorous. However, if you find facial expression hard to interpret and eye contact uncomfortable it might be making it harder (rather than easier) to communicate.

The monotropism theory of autism (see Murray *et al*, 2005; Milton, 2017) suggests that all of us have a limited amount of attention we can utilise at any one time. As autistic people may struggle to filter information if there is too much of it, or if an autistic person is particularly sensitive to whatever is happening, a useful strategy is to focus in on what is predictable and controllable. Therefore not looking someone in the eyes frees up attention and perceptual capacity to listen to what someone else is saying more intently (or vice versa).

Rule 5: Try to get a mismatch between your verbal and non-verbal communication

Autistic people might have difficulties in being able to read and interpret facial expressions and body language. Equally, it might be difficult to work out what an autistic person is thinking or feeling by just looking at facial expressions and body language. The chances of breakdowns in communication are therefore often quite high.

It is important to check out interpretations you are making from facial expressions and body language where possible, either with the person themselves or with people who know the autistic person well. Some people might need you to tell them how you are feeling and to explain exactly why you are feeling that way.

Gestures are vague and difficult to understand. They are informal and meanings can change. If the autistic person needs additional help to understand verbal communication, instead of relying on gestures, it is better to think about more formal visual communication systems such as photos, signed communication and objects of reference.

Rule 6: Always be vague and obscure

The English language has many idiosyncrasies and can be very confusing. English also has many phrases and sayings that can be difficult to understand unless you actually know what they are referring to (e.g. someone asking you to pull your socks up means 'do better than you have been doing' – unless of course your socks have come down …). Some, though not all, autistic people find irony or sarcasm confusing and are not sure whether to interpret what is said literally.

Autistic people might find it difficult to work out how much information to give. It is important to be as specific as possible and to find a way to make it clear how much information is required. Do you want a yes/no answer or more than that? It can be helpful to keep questions short and specific, so that it is clear from your question what exactly you are interested in finding out. For example, think about the question 'How did you get on today'? Are you asking about a specific part of the day or activity? It would be better to be specific e.g. 'Was there a lot of traffic?' 'Where did you eat your dinner'?. You can then ask follow-up questions. Instead of asking 'How are you?' you could ask 'Did you like...?'

Communication that is clear and direct might help to decrease misunderstandings.

Rule 7: Insist on interacting with me whenever you want to and pay no attention to my actions and wishes

Everyone has a need to control the amount of interaction, where it takes place, what it is about and who it takes place with. Finding out what the autistic person is interested in is a good place to start. What are likely to be good times or good topics?

We are all different in terms of the amount of interaction we enjoy. Some people go on holiday and relish the thought of meeting new people. For others, holidays are a good opportunity to get away from people.

Sudden interactions are likely to be more difficult, particularly if the autistic person is focusing on something else. Time to prepare is likely to help. For example, explaining what you want to talk about and how long for. Of course, this is not always possible for more informal interactions but nobody should be forced to take part in an interaction. It isn't the case that people should be 'made' to interact more if they find it difficult and that 'they will get used to it'. It is preferable to spend time working out better ways of interacting.

Rule 8: Ignore me

It is not ok to just ignore an autistic person. We all need repeated opportunities to engage in successful interactions. If your experience of interactions was that they were mostly hard work and unsuccessful and unpleasant, how willing might you be to engage in interactions in the future? If you keep trying to do something that is very hard to do, you might eventually give up and avoid situations that are so difficult.

Think about what the autistic person might want and need. There might be times when people really do want to be on their own and that is fine. This doesn't mean that the person never wants to interact with anyone. If you find it difficult to interact with an autistic person and don't understand some of his or her ways of behaving, find out more information. It may be that the autistic person behaves in a particular way when they are stressed and anxious or happy.

Try to be predictable. Make sure you allow plenty of time. Allow the autistic person to finish what they are doing first.

Rule 9: Demean me

Autistic people are all too often targeted for bullying and hate crime (Richardson *et al*, 2016), but also what might be considered 'micro-aggressions' against their way of being and self-esteem. Demeaning an autistic person is only going to feed into this negative narrative and potentially traumatise them further.

It is never ok to use derogatory language to describe someone's attempts at interaction and communication. Autistic people are likely to have experienced communication breakdown. This may have been very frequent. Autistic people may find it difficult to work out why a specific interaction has broken down (as might you) and might experience high levels of stress.

Respond to all attempts to communicate with encouragement and find good strategies to deal with communication breakdown. Start from the premise that people have very good reasons for doing what they do (or don't do). Support all attempts to communicate, whatever mode of communication is used. Create an environment where it is possible to have easy access to other forms of communication (signs, symbols, photos, written words, electronic communication aids etc.).

Rule 10: Don't make any adaptations – just treat me the same as you treat everyone else

Sometimes people can think that we make it harder for autistic people to communicate in the 'real world' if we make lots of adaptations to their home environment. This is not the case. The more experience we have of being able to both be understood and understand others, the more levels of stress are reduced and confidence increases (and probably our tolerance of communication breakdown increases too).

Make as many adaptations you can. Autism-friendly environments (where there is clear structure, positive expectations and experiences, empathy, low arousal and the opportunity to make links) are beneficial for everyone! The consequences of not getting this right for an autistic person tend to be much more severe and may mean that the person is not able to function and use the skills that they have.

References and further reading

Bartlett C & Bunning K (1997) The importance of communication partnerships: a study to investigate the communicative exchanges between staff and adults with learning disabilities. *British Journal of Learning Disabilities* **25** 148–153.

Beadle-Brown J, Roberts R & Mills R (2009) Person-centred approaches to supporting children and adults with autism spectrum disorders. *Tizard Learning Disability Review* **14** (3) 18–26.

Bell R (2012) "Does he have sugar in his tea?" Communication between people with learning disabilities, their carers and hospital staff. *Tizard Learning Disability Review* **17** (2) 57–63.

Bradshaw J (2000) A total communication approach towards meeting the communication needs of people with learning disabilities. *Tizard Learning Disability Review* **5** (1) 27–30.

Bradshaw J (2001) Complexity of staff communication and reported level of understanding skills in adults with intellectual disability. *Journal of Intellectual Disability Research* **45** (3) 233–243.

Bradshaw J (2011) Communication and challenging behaviour. In: S Hardy and J Theresa (Eds) *Challenging Behaviour: A handbook* (pp49–56). Brighton: Pavilion Publishing & Media.

Bradshaw J (2013) Communication and interviewing. In: E Chaplin, S Hardy and L Underwood (Eds) *Autism Spectrum Conditions: A guide* (pp129–141). Brighton: Pavilion Publishing & Media.

Bradshaw J (2013) The use of augmentative and alternative communication apps for the iPad, iPod and iPhone: an overview of recent developments. *Tizard Learning Disability Review* **18** (1) 31–37.

Bradshaw J, Beadle-Brown J, Richardson L, Leigh J & Whelton R (2016) *People on the autism spectrum who have intellectual disabilities: How do people communicate and what support do they get?* Paper presented at Autism Europe Conference, Edinburgh.

Communication Matters Journal (2013) volume 27 (3): https://www.communicationmatters.org.uk/sites/default/files/downloads/cmjournals/cmj_vol_27_no_3.pdf

Grove N (2015) Finding the sparkle: storytelling in the lives of people with learning disabilities. *Tizard Learning Disability Review* **20** (1) 29–36.

Hagan L & Thompson H (2014) It's good to talk: developing the communication skills of an adult with an intellectual disability through augmentative and alternative communication. *British Journal of Learning Disabilities* **42** 66–73.

Johnson H, Douglas J, Bigby C & Iacono T (2012) Social interaction with adults with severe intellectual disability: having fun and hanging out. *Journal of Applied Research in Intellectual Disabilities* **25** 4 329–341.

Milton D (2017) *Mismatch of Salience: Explorations of the nature of autism from theory to practice.* Brighton: Pavilion Publishing & Media Ltd.

Murray D, Lesser M & Lawson W (2005) Attention, monotropism and the diagnostic criteria for autism. *Autism* **9** (2) 139–156.

Porter J, Ouvry C, Morgan M & Downs C (2001) Interpreting the communication of people with profound and multiple learning difficulties. *British Journal of Learning Disabilities* **29** 12–16.

Thurman S, Jones J & Tarleton B (2005) Without words – meaningful information for people with high communication needs. *British Journal of Learning Disabilities* **33** 83–89.

Useful resources and websites

BILD *Hearing from the Seldom Heard*: http://www.bild.org.uk/about-bild/ourwork/seldom-heard/

Department of Health and Social Care *Making Written Information Easier to Understand* guidance: https://www.gov.uk/government/publications/making-written-information-easier-to-understand-for-people-with-learning-disabilities-guidance-for-people-who-commission-or-produce-easy-read-information-revised-edition-2010

Mencap's *Raising our Sights* communication guide: https://www.mencap.org.uk/sites/default/files/2016-06/2012.340%20Raising%20our%20sights_Guide%20to%20communication_FINAL.pdf

Murphy J & Cameron L (2006) *Talking Mats: A resource to enhance communication*. Stirling: University of Stirling.

Murphy J & Cameron L (2008) The effectiveness of Talking Mats® with people with intellectual disability. *British Journal of Learning Disabilities* **36** (4).

National Autistic Society, communication tips: http://www.autism.org.uk/about/communication/communicating.aspx

National Autistic Society, visual supports:
http://www.autism.org.uk/visualsupports

Royal College of Speech and Language Therapists
guidance: https://www.rcslt.org/news/good_
comm_standards

Personal communication passports: http://www.
communicationpassports.org.uk/Home/

Talking Mats: https://www.talkingmats.com/

United Response communication resource:
https://issuu.com/unitedresponse1/docs/ur_
communication_resource

The Participatory Autism Research Collective
(PARC): www.PARCautism.co.uk

Useful training and development resources from Pavilion Publishing

A Mismatch of Salience: Explorations of the nature of autism from theory to practice
By Damian Milton

Hall of Mirrors - Shards of Clarity: Autism, neuroscience and finding a sense of self
By Phoebe Caldwell

Choosing Autism Interventions: A Research-Based Guide
Bernard Fleming, Elisabeth Hurley and The Goth

Understanding Autism: A training pack for support staff and professionals based on 'Postcards from Aspie World'
By Dan Redfearn, Holly Turton, Hayden Larder and Helen Larder

Autism Spectrum Conditions: A guide

By Eddie Chaplin, Steve Hardy, Lisa Underwood

Autism and Intellectual Disability in Adults Volume 2

Dr Damian Milton and Professor Nicola Martin

Understanding and Supporting Children and Adults on the Autism Spectrum

By Julie Beadle-Brown and Richard Mills

Ten Rules for Ensuring People with Learning Disabilities and Those Who Are on the Autism Spectrum Develop 'Challenging Behaviour'... and maybe what to do about it

By Damian Milton, Richard Mills and Simon Jones

Ten Rules for Delivering a Diagnosis of Autism or Learning Disabilities in a Way That Ensures Lasting Emotional Damage ... and maybe what to do about it

By Viki Ainsworth and Jim Blair

Ten Rules for Ensuring Autistic People and People with Learning Disabilities Can't Access Healthcare...and maybe what to do about it

By Viki Ainsworth and Jim Blair